Light and Dark

POEMS BY

Barbara Howes

Wesleyan University Press

MIDDLETOWN, CONNECTICUT

Certain of these poems have appeared in: *In the Cold Country* (Bonacio & Saul with Grove Press, 1954); and in the following periodicals and anthologies: *Botteghe Oscure* (Rome), *Harper's Bazaar, Ladies' Home Journal, Modern Verse in English 1900– 1950,* edited by Lord David Cecil and Allen Tate (Macmillan, 1958), *New Poems by American Poets No. 2* (Ballantine Books, 1957), *The New Republic, New World Writing No. 8, Optique* (Port-au-Prince), *Le Petit Matin* (Tunis), *Poetry, La Posta Litteraria* (Lodi), *Saturday Review, The Sewanee Review, The Virginia Quarterly Review,* and *Voices.* The poems "On a Bou- gainvillæa Vine at the Summer Palace" (under the title of "On a Bougainvillæa Vine in Haiti"), "Early Supper," "Mistral," and "The Gallery," appeared originally in *The New Yorker.*

Library of Congress Catalog Card Number: 59–12478
Manufactured in the United States of America
First edition

Contents

I

LIGHT AND DARK

II

THE TRIUMPHS

III

IN THE COLD COUNTRY

I

LIGHT AND DARK

For Harriott Allen

Chimera

After a fearful maze where doubt
Crept at my side down the terrible lightless channel,
I came in my dream to a sandspit parting
Wind-tossed fields of ocean. There,
Lightstepping, appeared
A trio of moose or mules,
Ugly as peat,
Their trotters slim as a queen's.
"Hippocampi!" cried a voice as they sped
Over black water, their salty course,
And away. From the heaving sea
Then sprang a fabulous beast
For its evening gallop.
Head of a lion, goat's head rearing
Back, derisive, wild—the dragon
Body scaling the waves; each reckless
Nature in balance, flying apart
In one. How it sported
Across the water, how it ramped and ran!
My heart took heart. Awaking, I thought:
What was disclosed in this vision
Was good; phantom or real,
I have looked on a noble animal.

Early Supper

Laughter of children brings
    The kitchen down with laughter.
While the old kettle sings
Laughter of children brings
To a boil all savory things.
    Higher than beam or rafter,
Laughter of children brings
    The kitchen down with laughter.

So ends an autumn day,
    Light ripples on the ceiling,
Dishes are stacked away;
So ends an autumn day,
The children jog and sway
    In comic dances wheeling.
So ends an autumn day,
    Light ripples on the ceiling.

They trail upstairs to bed,
    And night is a dark tower.
The kettle calls: instead
They trail upstairs to bed,
Leaving warmth, the coppery-red
    Mood of their carnival hour.
They trail upstairs to bed,
    And night is a dark tower.

To W. H. Auden
on his Fiftieth Birthday

Books collide—
Or books in a library do:
Marlowe by Charlotte Mew,
Sir Horace Walpole by Hugh;
The most unlikely writers stand shoulder to shoulder;
One studies incongruity as one grows older.

Symbols collide—
Signs of the zodiac
Range the celestial track,
Pisces has now swung back
Into the lead: we learn to recognize
Each fleck for what it is in our mackerel skies.

Ideas collide—
As words in a poem can.
The poet, Promethean,
Strikes fire in a single line,
Form glows in the far reaches of his brain;
Poets who travel will come home again.

Feeling collides—
Lying for years in wait,
May grope or hesitate.
Now let us celebrate
Feeling, ideas, symbols, books which can
Meet with greatness here within one man.

Danaë

Golden, within this golden hive
Wild bees drone,
As if at any moment they may
Swarm and be gone
From the arched fibres of their cage,
Lithe as whalebone.

Over a pasture, once, I saw
A flock of small
Martins flying in concert, high
Then wheeling, fall;
Like buckshot pent in a string bag
They dotted all

That sky-patch, holding form in their flight,
A vase poured,
Their breathing shape hung in the air—
Below, the road
Fled secretly as quicksilver:
My eyes blurred.

All things come to their pinnacle
Though landscapes shift,
Women sit in the balance, as
Upon a knife;
Irony cuts to the quick—is this
Life or new life?

They sit their years out on a scale,
The heavy yoke
Of their heavy stomachs grounding them—
Or else come back

To barrenness with each full moon;
Minds go slack

Longing, or dreading, that a new
Form will take shape.
(The martins' swarming is a brush-stroke
On the landscape,
Within their white-gold, fleshly hall
The wild bees wake.)

Homing at close of day, they meet
This moment: now:
Love calls from its subterranean passage,
The bed they know
May support agony or joy—
To bed they go.

Midwinter Flight

Enclosed within its journey, the plane
Lies like the hull of a ship balanced
On ways of air, a war canoe
Jutting into the dark,
A radiant toy
Loosed upon space.
                    Here in this great cocoon
We passengers are pharaohs walled up
With honey, ambergris, grain and silver
To solace our hibernation.
Or we may be
Glazed ceramic fruit, a still-life
Kept for some later century
Under glass.
                    Now while the plane
Tunnels the black massif, we think of other
Things: a circular stair,
Drums, a crimson maple, rainfall, hills,
And checkered moths
Trembling on a lighted pane.

Cat on Couch

My cat, washing her tail's tip, is a whorl
Of white shell,
As perfect as a fan
In full half-moon . . . Next moment she's a hare:
The muzzle softens, rounds, goes dumb, and one
Tall ear dips, falters forward . . . Then,
Cross as switches, she's a great horned owl;
Two leafy tricorned ears reverse, a frown
Darkens her chalky visage, big eyes round
And round and stare down midnight.
                           There sits my cat
Mysterious as gauze,—now somnolent,
Now jocose, quicksilver from a dropped
Thermometer. When poised
Below the sketched ballet-
Dancers who pirouette upon the wall,
Calmly she lifts the slim
Boom of her leg, what will
The prima ballerina next
Perform?—Grace held in readiness,
She meditates, a vision of repose.

Lignum Vitæ

There in Bologna eighty saints are lodged
On pedestals, in rows up
The vaulted ceiling, till
Heads meet at the top
Of the hall.

Statues can wither like a blighted tree,
The hand holding the pen suffers
Dry rot, and a mantle embroidered
So skillfully
On oak

Disappears. Indeed, it is our loss
Not to have lived five hundred years
Ago, when in their vigor
These figures were all
One color.

A controversy now in black and white,
The restored saints look down: one's right
Hand is clean new pine,
Another's torso
Speckled

As a mosaic. Near the end is an old man
Reading a new book; his robe
Flows yet from broad shoulders
Without break
Or stain.

For a Florentine Lady

I

At death's door: how is it—
On the edge of that old mountain, looking out
Through windows of a darkened villa
On and on, far across Florence? Mist—
Insatiable and dull—
Hoods the ground, and those
Loved and clean-cut forms go shapeless,
Dim. Dear Lady,
Can we then help you move
Through realms of mist
By seeing you so clear,
Who greeted us erect and sure?

II

At death's door: how was it—
From the final edge of suffering, looking back
On all the sunlit, terraced years,
Back and back, far across Europe? Death—
Insatiable and cruel—
Stabbed the air, and those
Loved and clean-cut forms went shapeless,
Fell. Dear Lady,
Could we have helped you move
Through realms of dark
By seeing you so clear,
Who greeted us erect and sure?

City Afternoon

Far, far down
The earth rumbles in sleep;
Up through its iron grille,
The subway, black as a chimney-
Sweep, growls. An escalator rides
On dinosaur spines
Toward day. And on beyond,
Old bones, bottles,
A dismantled piano, sets
Of Mrs. Humphrey Ward all whirl
In the new disposal-unit; above
Its din, apartments are tenanted
Tight as hen-houses, people roosting
In every cupboard. Eighty storeys
Up, pigeons nest on the noise
Or strut above it; higher,
The outcast sun serves its lean meat
Of light.

The whinnying
Of Venetian blinds has ceased: we sit
Invisible in this room,
Behind glass. In a lull,
A chance abatement of sound, a scalping
Silence, far
Down we hear the Iron
Maiden whisper,
Closing upon her spikes.

Portrait of the Boy as Artist

Were he composer, he would surely write
A quartet for three orchestras, one train:
After the penny-whistle's turn, he might—
With ten bull-fiddles purring the refrain—
Dub in a lion to outroar the night.

Were he a painter, he would loose such bolts
Of color as would scare the sun, abash
Rainbows: a palomino-coated colt
Gallops on every speckled plain: a gashed
Knee bleeds rubies: frogs are emerald.

Were he a poet with the gift of tongues,
He'd scale the Andes in a metaphor,
Race Theseus in the labyrinth, among
Larks and angels act as troubadour,
For Daniel Boone shout at the top of his lungs.

Clear-eyed he sallies forth upon the field,
Holding close to his ear the shell of the world.

Home Leave

With seven matching calfskin cases for his new suits—
Wife and three children following up the plank—
The Colonel shepherds his brood on board.

As the band pumps out "Arrivederci
Roma," the airman's apple
Face bobs over the first-class rail;
Across the watery gap, Sicilian
Crowds like lemmings rush at the narrowing pier.

Poised on the balls of his feet, the athlete
Goes below. Headwaiters
Screen him with menus; sommeliers
Approach on the double; corks pop to the creaking
Of timbers, while he dreams
Of winning every ship's pool.

Florid, the airman bunts
Favors around the dance floor: sky-blue-pink
Balloons doze on the air. It is the Captain's
Dinner; haloed in streamers, he romps
With a Duchess and wins
At Musical Chairs.

Later, on the boat-deck, laced
Tight as a hammock by Irish
Whiskey, the athlete nuzzles the nurse. Collapsed
Like a tent around her, he rolls
With the ship.

After breakfast, the children on deck, New York
Near, balling his fists, the hero
Turns on his wife:
He hits out as if to do her honor.

With seven matching calfskin cases for his new suits—
Wife and children following down the plank—
The Colonel shepherds his brood ashore.

In forest-green sportcoat and desert brogans, he passes
Through Customs like quicksilver. His wife
Is heavily veiled; her three
Children follow like figures in effigy.

Tramontana

Down from the north,
Clearing the hill's
Snow-topped shoulder,
Lashing the pale
Brittle grass,
The wind wheels.

Skimming the land
Low, like a sickle,
Shaking the trees
Barren that feel
Its vehement breath,
Taunting the bells'
Tranquil high
Calm as they peal
Notes like moons,
The wind growls
In mock singsong.

Arguing all
Day, all night
Plaguing, the dull
River of sound
Rises, fills
Our being, and mind
Taut as a sail
Snaps: in its
Continual bellow
We choke, drown;
The wind kills.

Sirocco

Wind? This is no wind
Jaunty or wild like the others—
A substance buffing the skin—

This is a toad's wind:
Cantankerous and dull,
Irresolute, our brains

Are waterlogged; we quarrel
Spitting out yellow dust,
Ugly as puffballs

In the mustard-colored day;
Slack as a toad, our bleached
Land shimmers under its brassy

Sky. Amphibian green,
The warm consumptive air
Lowers, and will not turn

Inside out to keen and blow!
Fruit rots upon the vine;
The heart may start to mildew,

Rage take us by the throat,
Blood scald the eye until,
Stifling, we fall apart

Down to a lesser world.
This wind that hates the mind
Squats on till all is soiled.

Mistral

Percussive, furious, this wind
Sweeps down the mountain, and
Under its pennon of skirling air
Blows through each red-tiled house as if
Nothing were there: Mistral,
Quartz-clear, spread-eagle,
Falls on the sea.
Gust upon gust batters
The surface—darkening blue—
Into a thousand scalloped fans. Where
Shall our noontime friends,
Cicada, hummingbird,
Who stitched the air with sound and speed,
Now hide? All rocks, islands, peninsulas
Draw near, hitch up their chairs,
Companions in this clearer, clean
Air, while inland fields are stripped of soil.
As I start home, a coven
Of winds is let loose at every corner;
Alone in a howling
Waste, figurehead sculptured in air,
Bent low, deafened, I plunge
On, blind in the eye of the storm.

Ballade of the Inventory: In Provence

Crying havoc through its recumbent
Oval mouth, the chandelier
Is, from below, a virulent
Iron mask; to one less near,
Indifferent, it becomes a mere
Distasteful fixture, number nine
Marked on the inventory here,
While the wind harries the great pine.

Item: one terrace with cement
Flooring, a locked armoire, five clear
Panes—*en guillotine*—a bent
Brass curtain rod, nine rings, a fear
Of things unlisted, a chiffonier
That teeters; two sponge-racks, one tine
Missing; all form a lavaliere—
While the wind harries the great pine—

Or silken noose. What treasure spent,
What pride of possession, on this gear
Dusty, dimmed, impermanent,
Provisional. When nothing's dear
To anyone alive, a queer
Mélange remains. The sweet woodbine
Flaunts from a wall its green revere,
While the wind harries the great pine.

Etched poet of Provence, veneer
Peeling from your frame, we drink this wine
To do you honor. Could you but hear,
While the wind harries the great pine!

In Autumn

Redmen come
Lounging in pale sedans and
Then, at some entrance to the wilderness,
Dismount. Storming
Hill after hill,
Redcoated irregulars march,
Holding their guns like flagpoles;
Flannel men, pocketing small game,
Stamp through our threadbare wood . . .

Then head for home,
Guns at half-mast
For the carcass roped to the hood
Of the pale sedan.
Horns hook out over a headlight,
Nostrils drip
Blood on the fender, eyeballs bulge
At death. The male emblem is red.
Does that car not bear
Sorry insignia: brown,
On a field of pastel,
A stag dormant, antlered?

The Gallery

Into an empty cube
We step: the gallery,
Hung with ivory walls, lies still
As a squash court foundered in depths of sea.
Like players entering, we stare
Above the horizon line to where
Each opulent canvas, back to wall,
Confronts the room.
                And then gaze on till sight
Flickers, and vision swims
In an emulsion of color, till down
Their cones of intervening air
The chipped-glass fragments form and blur.
Paintings upon four walls—nothing alive
But painting. When we have gone,
Pictures in their magnificence remain,
Tranquil as spring looking in at an open window
On an empty room.

Death of a Vermont Farm Woman

Is it time now to go away?
July is nearly over; hay
Fattens the barn, the herds are strong,
Our old fields prosper; these long
Green evenings will keep death at bay.

Last winter lingered; it was May
Before a flowering lilac spray
Barred cold for ever. I was wrong.
　　　　　　　Is it time now?

Six decades vanished in a day!
I bore four sons: one lives; they
Were all good men; three dying young
Was hard on us. I have looked long
For these hills to show me where peace lay . . .
　　　　　　　Is it time now?

A Lullaby

Landlocked, the child
Stirs, its curtained chamber
Blood-red in the blind dark, somnolent as amber;
Stirs: yet still the human
Alembic admits no change
But, tight in its leathern skin,
Climbs upon a landing
Where espaliered on the walls,
Doubled, the past dissolves
In two mirroring lanes. Yet all
Must come to birth. Can we
Reflecting the future, follow it there? Oh,
Landlocked, the child
Stirs, and will be born!

Tea in the Garden

She saw her visitor.
Wind in the branches, gust
On gust, above them swayed
The grape arbor—vines hung
Disheveled as old hair
Tight-crimped and stiff, the dried-
Out tendrils like fine wire.
She sat still. Her mottled
Hand—crisscrossed, the leaves
A sieve to filter light—
Wavered toward her cup,
Her gaze rejoined the vacant
Air. Memory is an arch
Before which pose charades
Out of the past, round, bronzed
By time: arch on arch—
As wickets for croquet
Set by some giant—lent
A huge perspective; clear
On at the end a slate
Wall, chalked on the rising
Night; below, the lozenged
Green coffers of the sea.
Blindly she turned, bestowed
Her aging rictus. Gates
About them clanged shut, clanged:
"Welcome, you are my guest."

L'Ile du Levant: The Nudist Colony

All the wide air was trawled for cloud
And then that mass confined in a grey net
And moored to the horizon. Bowed

Down, the golden island under
A dull sky was not at its best; its heyday
Is when the heat crackles, the sun

Pours like a boiling waterfall
On matted underbrush and thicket, on
Boulder, dust; and, over all,

Cicadas at their pastime, drilling
Eyelets of sound, so many midget Singer
Sewing machines: busy, then still.

Landing beyond a thorny curve
We climbed down to the colony, extended
On its plot of beach. In the sudden swerve

Of every eye, they saw as one,
These Nudists on vacation, half their days
Prone, determined as chameleons

To match the ground beneath. At ease
Within a sandy cage, they turned to stare
Up at us clad identities

Who came to stare as openly
As if we too had railings fore and back
And the whole mind of a menagerie.

Such freedom of the flesh, if brave,
Lacks subtlety: a coat of sunburn can
Be badly cut. Well-tailored love

Not only demonstrates but hides,
Not only lodges with variety
But will keep private its dark bed.

We rose: below us golden-brown
Bodies of young and old, heavy and lean,
Lay beached upon the afternoon.

While water, casual as skin,
Bore our departing boat, we saw a form
In relief against the rocky line

And stood to wave farewell from our
World to his, even as charcoal dusk
Effaced his lazy semaphore.

II

THE TRIUMPHS

For Milton Saul

The Triumph of Time

    . . . Mounted on its triumphal chariot, Earth,
Shawled with the changing seasons, casts them off
In execution of a solemn dance:

Valleys the snow has leveled sink with spring
And hills start upward on a wave of green,
Warm winds sweep down on fallow pastures . . . How
Easily summer conquers: liberal,
It broods upon the world as a trapeze
Hangs poised above its long trajectory.
Autumn: a crazy hunter comes to poach
Inflaming all upon a zigzag path
Magenta, tangerine—the woods are torn
Asunder. Soon an old man whose mackintosh
Flaps about narrow flanks, will quit the house
And, hourglass in hand, check the sundial.
Old Doge, old Cupid, the sun at your time of year
Is pale as death;—and is it death that comes,
Darkening the wind?
              Although the dance would seem
To have reached its end, still clockwise earth will swing,
In each triumphant season witnessing
How this, this temporal dance, breaks from eternal
    love. . . .

The Triumph of Chastity

Over the plain two dark
Equestrian figures pound
Charging full tilt at spring;
Behind them burnt-over ground,
A desolate panel stretches,
A long dun scarf unwound.

The taller, Cavalier
Hatred, his horny gut
Wild with the heat of their ride
Spurs onward, faster yet
Must he race his mighty Arab
Stallion; upon her jennet

Side-saddle, stride for stride,
Gallops the Lady, fleet
Ambition; her sallow hair
Streams on the wind like light,
Cold as a cameo
Her face. They sow a great

Swathe of the plain with dust;
On, on he presses. Now,
Mantles like bellying sails,
They scud at the wood, and so
Storm forward till he reins in,—
Midnight upon his brow,

Caparisoned in jet,
Harness, panache of black
Spume-flecked, his stallion's eye
Encrimsoned;—they rein back
To their haunches the quivering steeds
At the brink:—Scrub, tamarack,

Meadows defoliate,
Autumnal. They who have
Outrun the spring, now halt
To seek as in a cheval-
Glass one eternal face.
Each stares at his own self-love.

The Triumph of Love

As from some grand
Venetian ballroom ceiling
Veronese's cupids
Gaze
Down, ringed
About the cupola,
Coronas of bright hair
Encircling them with light, suspended
There, clipped sturdy wings
Folded, chin in hand
Or holding tight the attic balcony which like
The top rung of a ladder wells
Dizzily above us who look up,
Heads thrown back, craning, seeking our
Reflected stare:

So toward the sleeping child do we
Converge,
Eyelids lowered and look down,
Once more so moved that all
Space dwindles
And the Palace walls
Are scaled to inches by our deepening love.

The Triumph of Death

Illusion forms before us like a grove
Of aspen hazing all the summer air
As we approach a new plateau of love.

With discs of light and shade, vibration of
Leaf-candelabra, dim, all-tremulous there,
Illusion forms before us like a grove

And bends in welcome: with each step we move
Nearer, quick with desire, quick to dare.
As we approach a new plateau of love,

New passion, new adventure wait above
And call to our drumming blood; all unaware
Illusion forms before us like a grove

In a mirage, we reach out to take Love
In our arms, compelled by one another's stare.
As we approach a new plateau of love

The aspen sigh in mockery: then have
We come this way before? Staining the air,
Illusion forms before us like a grove
As we approach a new plateau of love.

The Triumph of Pride

Not to retain,
Not to let go;
Not to approve—

Even of the blue heron
That soars and is gone—
Of anyone

Giving pleasure or pain—
Flown away so
Quickly, like love.

The Triumph of Truth

Speaking out of a clear sky
I greeted two people at once; perhaps my eye
Saw less the real than the imagined figure.
These two repassed, rhythmically, like a fan,
Or like two dancers swaying
Apart, then eclipsing the other.

In an old painting Truth is drawn
In triumph by two elephants: a woman
Holding a great sword and a golden book,
While all around her, kings, philosophers,
And poets in her train
Nod and debate again.

How the rude sun has bronzed their skin!
See how her jeweled book reflects the inner
Light of their noble faces, of their crowns.
Truth's jet-black broadsword shudders over all,
An iron ruler poised,
That suddenly may sweep down.

Out of a clear sky Art speaks
The truth; two dancers separate and mix;
Each of us is an atoll whose protective
Shell is hard. But, a true mariner,
Art looks far out, and Truth
In triumph rides, with Love.

IN THE COLD COUNTRY

For Ximena de Angulo

Primavera

The horse with consumption coughed like the end
        of the world.
We heard its tremblors echo in that dry bark,
But on our carriage rolled; we minted miles,
Like hoops our coined wheels rolled until the dark
Came down upon the city, and grey shade
Merged all the cathedral's zebra stripes; the park
Recessed for night, vendors' flags, bird-wings furled.

Onward and on we rode until the dawn.
From jeweled opera-box and catacomb
We summoned up the past: released, the ghosts
Came forth in cloth of gold and tilting heaume
In every city street and hornèd lane
Whose flowers pell-mell hung down, geranium foam
From walls all staunch with red, red staunched by stone.

And on and on; where would the journey end?
Giotto conceived a tower in pure air,
Heraldic rainbow; balanced on her shell
All beauty woke in Aphrodite fair
As history's fairest. Now to trespassers
On the volcano's flank the tocsins blare:
Our mare's obsidian hooves foreknelled the end.

Portrait of an Artist

For dear life some do
Many a hard thing,
Train the meticulous mind
Upon meaning, seek
And find, and yet discard
All that is not of reality's tough rind.

A cool divining rod,
The heart, another tool,
Keen as a hawk's eye,
Supple as water, bends
Responsive to all four
Humors. In many sympathy runs dry

Or blots and blurs. To be
Ascetic for life's sake,
Honest and passionate,
Is rare. I think of those
Images of Buddha placed
In shells, and later found encased in pearl.

Light and Dark

Lady, take care; for in the diamond eyes
Of old old men is figured your undoing;
Love is turned in behind the wrinkled lids
To nurse their fear and scorn at their near going.
Flesh hangs like the curtains in a house
Long unused, damp as cellars without wine;
They are the future of us all, when we
Will be dried-leaf-thin, the sour whine
Of a siren's diminuendo. They have no past
But egg-husks shattered to a rubbish heap
By memory's looting. Do not follow them
To their camp pitched in a cranny, do not keep
To the road for them, a weary weary yard
Will bring you in; that beckoning host ahead,
Inn-keeper Death, has but to lift his hat
To topple the oldster in the dust. Read,
Poor old man, the sensual moral; sleep
Narrow in your bed, wear no
More so bright a rose in your lapel;
The spell of the world is loosed, it is time to go.

The Heart of Europe

See the crazy gate
Or crazy house atilt, terraced with air
Where solid wall once stood, cliff-dwellers' home.
Or here a man,
A soldier once, night-watching out the day,
Life's blinders are put on him young.
He sells
Pencils, we turn away; the penny price
Is too great for this sideshow of a world;
Pity, a flea-bite, fades.
A witch's brew
May have reduced all to a crazy-quilt,
A patchwork satire on the grace of man,
So limber in the grace of God
He, mountebank animal, makes his cities silt
Overnight. The eye of newt, bull's ear,
Blood of an infant born within wedlock,
Alchemy's golden key, the soldiers' cube
Of sustenance, all these have wreaked a spell
Every old woman mumbles endlessly.
Whether we brood or work or sit
Vacant and staring, how the cold March winds
Blow through the defenceless houses, over the limp
Flags of laundry hung from the ruins,
Upon the helpless old, for all are old,
Freezing them in its icy tourniquet.
But yet throughout, hate grows, builds up to tower
A flaming Lucifer higher than the spires
Of the dark drugged cathedrals;
He bends down
In triumph over the wreckage of the town.

Goosegirl

Again the careless goose walks over my grave,
Again the splayed foot's echo radios ill
Toward me aswirl in the happy amphitheatre
Where love stood still.

This is the other side of passion, for
Our days careen in paradox; this toy,
My heart, is colder at white heat than ice,
A jeopardy of joy.

The dreadnought goose will tread its fill on us yet,
And semaphore foreknowledge of those drives
Toward love, of love, and all, all counterfeit,
Our carelong lives.

Everywoman

Oh where are you riding, lady,
So fast on your mindless horse?
What wonder has set the compass
That leads you this skyline course;
What goal or what comfort, lady,
Call with such force?

Oh where are you riding, riding?
For autumn burns in the eyes
Of those you pass so gaily
In your fresh greening guise;
The leaves have sickened, lady,
And their sap dries.

Oh where, oh where are you riding?
Your horse is a hollow gong
Whose hoofbeats fade to an echo
As thin as your wisp of song;
No flesh to your grasp, none, lady,
And the nights grow long.

The Stag of God

The neck of the white stag of the valley
Yearns toward the sky with such grace
That his soul can but continue this aspiration
Further in space;

Firm-moulded spire of ivory
Stretched up, up, as if to touch
The tenderest spiced leaves in Eden.
No distrust

Deepens the shadows of his eyes
Or sets the muscles of his sturdy shoulders
Jangling. The cool powerful basilica
Of his body holds

Firm in the agony of spring
And in the passion of the storm,
White and firm after all the years that crept
By his white form.

Yet the bleached stag of the valley
Has no shadow to cast upon the earth
To warm it, no full-throated gospel-call
To reach every hearth;

His mighty haunches hold but do not spring
Forward and outward in sympathy
Or penance; were he ever to regain
Sinew and elasticity

He might not, high and cold upon the land
Outworn as the poor Ark on Ararat,
Look useless down while the tormented world
Seeks past that spot.

Landscape and Figure

The concrete-colored sky
Loomed sullen overhead
As I, at the highway edge,
Scuffed out my private track
In the shale of the road's shoulder.
Each auto, a torpedo,
Sped through its tube of air;
I ran, but they fled past me
As if I were standing still,
Immobile as a scarecrow
Upon whose battered hat
All seasons, weathers fall.
These were two worlds, and speed
Was killer king; I feared
Each one might end my walking.

How strange the sleight-of-hand
Of memory, that I should
Recall, at such a time,
This Mughal painting: when
On Shah Jehan its curious
Shadow fell, must he
Not have rejoiced to feel
Marked by its beauty in
Intaglio? Here reigns
Color, landscape, form,
Rock, peacock, antelope
Composed on an emerald field;
While at the plane-tree's trunk
See how the tawny hunter
Barefoot mounts swift, the sky
Of golden light aglow

All about the ecstatic tree.
Emblazoned, embossed with green,
Scarlet and tourmaline,
Topaz, or leaves of brass,
It stands. The squirrel-prey,
Intent, bead-sharp their eyes,
Flirt dangerward their tails,
Then feint, like acrobats,
In tawny rivulets,
Flash deeper, to flash away
Behind the pendent leaves.

Color, color. Oh,
Was this picture dead in the real
Arterial vista, or was
This roadway a mirage,
A trick of vision? There
Lay only the cold March day,
The narrowing tarmac tape
And the saurian machines,
Whose deaf-mute drivers sat
Remote in their diamond aim,
As if they would run right out
Of time. The leaden street
Mirrored the sky; in fear
I turned back for my car.

The New Leda

Goosegirl, your feet are slow
And heavy with acceptance, while the echo
Of what will come
Gathers momentum and batters at your eardrum.

The future hangs
Over you like an airborne bell, its clangs
Will gut your heart, will keep
Up their reverberant assault, no sleep

Will be the same again;
Marked, muted by this inexorable hyphen
You cannot be the same;
There is no sanctuary, the god will come

And bed you in his plumage;
Intent, bird-lidded, knotted in his rage
Of lust he will flail down
Every abject appeal. . . . Quiet in gown

Of white the bride of Christ
Moves down the waiting nave as if her wrist
Were held and she led,
Hands heart obeying the seeing unseen Dead,

And she led on as though
Walking through shallow water, where the slow
Tide urges at her feet
But checks their driftwood longing. Will the sweet

Wan dedicated face,
Inward as some old painting, find a place
Of sweetest rest, a home
Now in the Spirit's mansion and catacomb?

Will she encounter love,
Laughter, pain and grief, or will she live
For centuries encased
In waterglass serenity; the taste

Of an eternal death
In life upon her lips, although breath
Cannot fail? Her
Limbo holds her like a fly in amber,

Beyond the reach of life.
Sisters, wastrels, when will you have enough
Of sacrifice and harm
And deprivation? Remember the mighty arm

That, white and sick with strain,
Wrestled the whole night out until the plain
Was light and he could see
Deep down the precipice of self, his adversary

And ask his blessing. Either
Make peace with yourselves, or live locked in such war
As, ruinous from the start,
Turns dark with pity Jacob's brazen heart.

Coq de Combat

There Jack-cock struts
Rattling his brassy plumage,
Gamey torso rearing,
Aims his beak
And then,
Oh-ho, lets loose a challenge
That, like darts,
Will smite the target ear,—
Coco-rico!

How can this cocky mobster know
That soon the tumbrils of the night
Will move to harvest darkness,
Or the stars
Like crocuses will close;
The Cyclops moon
All day must be put out,
Its eye interred
In a great vault blue as forget-me-not?

Our brave cock struts:
This very day
May be his day for battle
When, armed cap-à-pie,
All rapier beak and spurs,
Angry, leaping, he'll try
To blood-let and life-let his enemy.
Coco-rico!

Now he,
A feathered timepiece,
Monitor of dawn,
At this gargantuan ring presides,
In his turn bells us out
To do, endure, or die,—
Coco-rico!

In a Prospect of Flowers

Of a painter drowned in his twentieth year

As in his tomb
In amethystine water the artist lies,
Framed by raw cement, lapped
By many-petalled sunlight
That engraves
Each phosphorent particle.

He
Hangs there face down,
His body ominous in this design,
Dark head resting on the lapis-lazuli
Empty bosom of water,
Flung
Like Icarus.
Now no vision can again
Furnish those hands with vision
Or
That heart with color.

Royal palms,
The columns of some ancient portico,
Incline;
And we, downcast
At this imagined brink,
Lament and praise—
Within a fatal aquarelle—
The lineaments of the ideal.

Mirror Image: Port-au-Prince

Au petit
Salon de Coiffeur,
Monique's / hands fork
like lightning, like a baton
rise / to lead her client's hair
in *repassage:* she irons out the kinks.
Madame's brown cheek / is dusted over with a
paler shade / of costly powder. Nails and lips are red.

Her matching lips and nails incarnadined, / in the
next booth Madam consults her face / imprisoned
in the glass. Her lovely tan / is almost
gone. Oh, watch Yvonne's astute
conductor fingers set the
permanent, / *In little*
Drawing-room of
Hairdresser!

The Sport of Boys

Seeing the wild boys on the beach,
The cruel waves strike the shore,
From far in a small boat
Where the long draw
Up and fall of waters
Lulled us, slow
Tides beneath and all
At anchor though
In motion. Seeing the waves'
Monotonous thrust
Upward on sand on crabs
Wetting the nests
Of leathery weathered weeds,
A great sower
Casting its watery seed
Upon the shore
In slow dispassionate rhythm
Only ceasing
When tides turn over.
Exultant ring
Of childish voices calls
Our eyes. They run
Up and down, with stout
Sticks flailing one
Slow crustacean after
Another, crushing—
Jackdaws beaked for havoc—
Destroying hurting
In ecstasy of pointless
Cruelty. God
Knows men love to kill:
Jesse's rod

Has turned into a club,
And we, far off,
Shocked, so far, our shout
Faint as a cough.

Relatives

Their eyes go out on stalks like crabs' to the closet;
Sipping their tea they uncoil a précis,
Rumours of shame, malfeasance, bizarre ills
Among the invisible family choir. They covet
Each out-turned glance, all hawsers loaned to land
As I move slowly waterward; they shock
And simper, crouching ringed upon the deck
Rattling the bony dice of tribal fate.
It is time, you jackanapes crew! The moon lets down
The shelled gold of her wake on the river ahead.
It is time to unpilot you; we shall not be late.

The Nuns Assist at Childbirth

Robed in dungeon black, in mourning
For themselves they pass, repace
The dark linoleum corridors
Of humid wards, sure in the grace

Of self-denial. Blown by duty,
Jet sails borne by a high wind,
Only the face and hands creep through
The shapeless clothing, to remind

One that a woman lives within
The wrappings of this strange cocoon.
Her hands reach from these veils of death
To harvest a child from the raw womb.

The metal scales of paradox
Tip here then there. What can the nun
Think of the butchery of birth,
Mastery of the flesh, this one

Vigorous mystery? Rude life
From the volcano rolls and pours,
Tragic, regenerate, wild. Sad
The unborn wait behind closed doors.

Death on the Platform

As the train moves,
The old man falls
To the hungry wheels.
There is none to aid,
To stop the machine
In its mineral round,
And the frozen earth
Is a cruel confederate.

A child will brave
A nonsensical
But painful spill
From his canting sled,
And on coming clean
Through, will not wonder
About his birth
Or auspice; but, elate,

Climb back, high above
His last perch: taller.
Yet such furies fill
Man's greying head
He must try to sign
Each leaf, confound
Doom with his breath,
To die, at the last, intestate.

The college grove
Where the Chancellor
Kept life at his heels,
Where all men made

Obeisance then
To the scarlet gown,
The rich red heart
Of their intellectual state,

Will lose his love.
He is stricken, all
Is so quickly still.
And the princedom held
With mind, with dream,
Panoply, power
Flees him at death
Who naked speaks of man's blind fate.

Morning-Glory

for C. W.

Now when spiralling summer burns
Its way toward autumn, on this vine
The morning-glory opens such
Buoyant parasols of blue,
Uplifted into light, as to
Recover spring . . . recovering much
More: the azure of a mind
And cloudless heart to which we turn.

In the Cold Country

We came so trustingly, for love, but these
Lowlands, flatlands, near beneath the sea
Point with their cautionary bones of sand
To exorcize, submerge us; we stay free
Only as mermaids glittering in the waves:
Mermaids of the imagination, young
A spring ago, who know our loveliness
Banished, like fireflies at winter's breath,
Because none saw; these vines about our necks
We placed in welcome once, but now as wreath
Against the scalpel cold; still cold creeps in
To grow like ivy over our chilling bodies
Into our blood. Now in our diamond dress
We wive only the sequins of the sea.
The lowlands have rejected us. They lie
Athwart the whispering waters like a scar
On a mirage of glass; the dooming land,
Where nothing can take root but frost, has won.
And what of warmth and what of joy? They are
Sequestered elsewhere, southward, where the sun
Speaks. For all our mermaid vigilance
And balance, all goes under; underneath
The land's grey wave we falter and fall back
To hibernate within the caves of death.

Views of the Oxford Colleges

Oxford abounds in fern and bird-watcher.
It is a lovely place when its short spring
Softens the chilblained air, and coats the stone
Tombs of buildings with its early green.
It is most lovely to the mind's eye
When age and earnestness discreetly sing.

Prudence and earnestness discreetly sing
Their muted canticles; the eighty odd
Year old, the old at twenty-five, or the
Intelligent wrapped in long mufflers nod
At beauty passing, but their baths are cold,
They have an ague and believe in God.

The ague holds, and the belief in God
Carries them through the valley of depression,
Bleak as any mine, like Cromwell who,
Roundheaded in his obstinacy, rang down
A curtain on felicity; the past
Is moored in Oxford firm as an obsession.

Moored in Oxford firm as an obsession,
Man opens his umbrella which will turn
Back the sensual sun; he cannot feel—
Poor dampened Adam—love or beauty burn
Caught within the spokes of that black wheel.
Oxford abounds in bird-watcher and fern.

The Don

A cockney rounds the corner, laundry pins
Upon his nose; a deathshead spouting Greek
Totters abaft the podium: dates of birth
And death sicken the air like blackboard chalk.
The words are mouthed and mumbled till they fall,
Shredded, behind his hand, in the long hall.
This is the scholiast's black mass; we sit
And fret to see each poem impaled, dead
As butterfly on pin, as dried egg-shell.
Necromancer of learning, a black bat
With wing extended over literature,
He sweeps to rend Adonis' living body.
Beauty is extinguished, value gone;
Silence in the hall; dark in the hall; all's done.

Indian Summer

This man, this stranger in my arms
Lies quiet now, below in sleep,
Lost in the deep seine of his dream.
How wide the net is cast, far out, far down,
But his dream plumbs himself; mine is my own.

Two feral figures in the jungle half-
Light taut in struggle
Shoulder to shoulder,
Cold hate, colder force
In the leashed clash of wrestlers
Clasped in war in
One another's arms;
There they enact
The ancient drama of possession.
But who has won?
Deep down within the womb
Of dream, of his own dream,
Each acts his part, and is by it possessed.

Time's horn of plenty spills
Out to us her dialectic
Changing forms;
No one can say
When love will take root,
Run wildfire up the heart's trellis. We
Harbor such diversity
That turning now we find
The future in our arms,
A golden cataract that comes
Out of the cornucopia of dream.

Lament

Often thinking of death one dreams of a river
Whose sensual waters, black as pitchblende, roll
Out as if powered, poured by some huge engine.
Light grazes the water, refracts; its depths are too old
For eye or for light to pierce. But death, the sure diver,

Cuts rapier-quick his element, and casts
Down all that his traveling touched. The waterlogged
Dead stuff of branch or animal floats by,
Insects skim, a visored turtle flogs
Its way along, eddies drink air and are lost.

We who stand on the bank in the luminous quiet
Of evening, our hands linked, sorrowing, face
The wilderness that waits beyond the river.
The wild cannot rest with the tame, the forest preys
Always upon its own to prey, and not

Till death come cradle them will they pause for peace.
We have read justice on what cannot change,
On nature pitched too high for harmony,
And so were right and wrong. And so the strange
Wild frantic clear-eyed ones are gone. Released

From their war with life now, on the breast of the river
We see them pass, and half the world is dressed
In sunlight's full regalia, while thunders rear
And clang their giant tympani; the west
Awaits its sun at the end of the impenetrable river.

The Critic

Ugolino takes his rest,
For rest he needs after such labor;
He has prepared a tasty stew
Neglecting neither sauce nor savor;
His spiritual fathers he has cooked,
Basted, spitted and sprigged with bay,
His cultural fathers he has eaten,
And now he's quite as great as they.
Great with father sitteth he
Happy, for they are no more:
Eliot, with thyme bedight,
Tossed like Leander to the shore;
Yeats tumbled to oblivion
Without a mourner; Ugolino
Surveys his future dancing bright
As Theda Bara at the Kino.
He wears contentment like a wreath
And for a smile an orange rind,
There is no art but in his belch
Whose stomach's bigger than his mind.

The Bar at the Carrousel

Cloche-hatted like Hermes, game-feathered for wings,
Emotion drives her body as one leans
Against the storm-swept tiller, features sharp
With rage and sting.

She sits there, perches, while her love, her friend,
Placed doll-like between her and the man
Revolves in coquetry, the prey of each,
Who both intend

That she shall wear their colors, turning now
To the distraught rouged mask, then to the man's
Jowled face, his eyes like pegs, but free in the world
To come or go.

The rioting heart of Sappho's stormy daughter
Sends out hate which even he can feel
Who takes his leave abruptly, caring little;
The usual slur

Of the world falls off like spray from a plunging bow.
She aches with triumph, and the muscles round
Her thin lips swell with power, a pretty death-
Mask quickening now.

In this museum, the world, we have a fine
Prospect of ancient gods, nor should we fail
To recognize here Hermes as death's agent.
The androgyne

At home in her half-world, woman's companion,
Seneschal among the shadows, waits
To guide her curving way until she wanders
All compass gone.

The Balcony

Light playing on the water plays on the trees,
Shimmers and scatters, dowering them with light.
All things partake of the sun's strength,
The long warm hand of heaven is on us until night.

As from a prow that juts in space we watch
Stipple of wind upon the quiet lake,
Each idle insect droning on,
And high above our heads see heron in echelon

Ferry across on deep unhurried wing.
All these foreshortened forms your eyes compose
And render to my understanding,
So that the sunlight too reflects your influence.

Such wisdom near me, I am nearer the light
Whose every incident you so endow.
This is immediacy, this is love;
And by its gracious hand I wake from darkest night.

Three Translations from the French

I

THE ROSES OF SA'ADI

(*Marceline Desbordes-Valmore*)

I wanted this morning to bring you a gift of roses,
But I took so many in my wide belt
The tightened knots could not contain them all

And burst asunder. The roses taking wing
In the wind were all blown out to sea,
Following the water, never to return;

The waves were red with them as if aflame.
This evening my dress bears the perfume still:
You may take from it now their fragrant souvenir.

II

EL DESDICHADO

(*Gérard de Nerval*)

The dark one am I, the widowed, unconsoled,
Prince of Aquitania whose tower lies ruined,
My one star is dead, and my radiant lute
Renders only the black sun of Melancholy.

In the night of the tomb, oh, you, my consoler,
Give me back Posilipo and the Italian sea,
The flower which delighted my desolate heart,
And the trellis where the vine and the roses marry.

Am I Eros or Phoebus, Lusignan or Biron?
My brow is still red with the kiss of the Queen;
I have dreamed in the grotto where the siren swims . . .

And twice have I, victor, crossed the Acheron:
Passing, in turn, on Orpheus' lyre
From the sighs of a saint to a fairy's cries.

III

The Lost Wine

(*Paul Valéry*)

One day into the sea I cast
(But where I cannot now divine)
As offering to oblivion,
My small store of precious wine . . .

What, oh rare liquor, willed your loss?
Some oracle half-understood?
Some hidden impulse of the heart
That made the poured wine seem like blood?

From this infusion of smoky rose
The sea regained its purity,
Its usual transparency . . .

Lost was the wine, and drunk the waves!
I saw high in the briny air
Forms unfathomed leaping there.

The Undersea Farmer

To dream of islands. . . .
The mind's eye moves and planes
Up the incline of sea,
They lie atilt there
Against the horizon. Islands

Are moored on shoals
And tower above the vaults
Of black water, pyramids
Of depth, where old
Benumbed seas chill the shoals;

What arteries
Of light shaft down these fathoms
At length snuff out in black,
The sea-pit water
Muffles even the arteries

Of the imagination
But as it muffles, fills.
Our tines touch depth and surface
As we roll
In our imagination,

In the sea,
In the glaucous sunny deep water
Between worlds. A shark
That goes his easy
Narrative through our sea,

Poses a model
Gesture in his here-
To-there progress, long
Curving pentameter
Of skaters; or note a model

Of the oblique in the flying
Fish's brushing shadow
While he high-tails it over
The waves; he grazes
Us only with his dark flying-

Away symbol
For our notebooks and hope and joy;
If we prefer the conceptual
Seahorse, he rides
The waves as if a symbol

Of inwardness mounted
There; flesh tucked beneath
His bony plates; all outline,
But motored
From within; my mounting

Wonder at such
Proliferation allows
But a glimpse at the shagreen
Sea urchin, delicate
As Christmas tree ornaments, such

Mystery in
Its being, one can only
Believe that it does breathe.
These denizens
Of form are catalysts in

Our minds; so let us go
Hand over hand back toward
The watery skylight, toward land,
Afraid only of letting
Our subaqueous lifeline go.

The Lost Girl

The wise Irish have it that the circle
Dew-marked in the deep sward is where
The little people danced: their fairy ring,
Their empery within this demarcation.
We cut our circles in the ice of rooms
Where by firelight two skaters glide
In friendship, courtship, hatred—for love or doom
Are they bound tighter in their circling
Till life can never be the same for each.
Or as any group, meeting at hazard, skiers,
Or housemaid and butler leveled below stairs,
Soon feel grow round them this retaining wall,
A group's invisible and plastic caul.

The girl from her charmèd circle has strayed away,
Incomprehensibly lost; we were all here,
In her subtraction everything is changed;
The face of the world is askew, fear knocks knocks knocks,
Our round floor tilts, we are queasy with questioning,
Dreading the answer, dreading we may not hear;
Walls crumble, we are shaken and spilled like eggs
In a wreck, all thrown, addled, of a sudden alone.
Days scud away, so by disaster blown.

The land, on a map, runs out secure and clear,
The effortless car disgorges, gorges miles,
But space has swollen, an enormity,
Each field is a decade, we falter, cold,
Seeing how many graves the ground can hold.

The circle is broken, splayed in the wide expanse
Of land, too far, too rough, too huge for search;
Has earth cracked open and swallowed her in its spasm?
Sky thunders down upon us, and we fall
Out of God's mouth, down into the reeling chasm.

Annunciation

Time, a recording angel, bends
One knee upon the grass:
There in the azure close of day
Remote against the arras
Of herb and floweret he broods
On what may come to pass.

Shadows of afternoon arrange
A cloak about her head;
Silent she stands beneath the groined
Portal, awaiting word
Or sign from that ghostly visitor
Of what will be her meed:

Will he say nothing, and she turn
Her back and go within?
Or, waxing, in a little while
Step out upon a scene
Of Tuscan summer, bearing proud
Contour of mandolin?

On a Bougainvillæa Vine
at the Summer Palace

Under the sovereign crests of dead volcanoes,
See how the lizards move in courtly play;
How when the regnant male
Fills the loose bagpipe of his throat with air,
His mate will scale
Some vine portcullis, quiver, halt, then peer—
Eyes sharp as pins—
At that grandee posed stiff with self-esteem,
His twiglike tail acurve.

What palaces lie hid in vines! She sees
Chameleon greenrooms opening on such
Elite boudoirs,
Flowers as bright as massacres; should she
Not try their spiring tendrils
That like string
Hammocks are slung upon the open air?
Tensing his tiny jaw, he seems to smile;
And while all nature sways,
Lightly rides his delicate trapeze.

A virid arrow parts
The leaves—she's at
His side. Then darts away; he following,
They lose themselves within the redolent shade. . . .
Quiet the palace lies
Under the sun's green thumb,
As if marauding winter would never come.

The Homecoming

All the great voyagers return
Homeward as on an arc of thought;
Home like a ruby beacon burns
As they crest wind, scale wave, soar air;
All the great voyagers return,

Though we who wait never have done
Fearing the piteous accidents,
The coral reef sharp as the bones
It has betrayed, fate's cormorant
Unleashed, whose diving's never done.

Even the voyager of mind
May fail beneath behemoth's weight;
Oh, the world's bawdy carcass blinds
All but the boldest, rots the sails
And swamps the voyaging of the mind.

But all the great voyagers return
Home like the hunter, like the hare
To its burrow; below, earth's axle turns
To speed their coming, the following fair
Winds bless their voyage, blow their safe return.